My Name is My Name and My Name CAN'T Change!

By: Michael Assivero

WTL INTERNATIONAL

My Name is My Name and My Name Can't Change

Artwork by Mohiul Islam Rony and Cutie Fruity by WTL

Published by
WTL International
930 North Park Drive
P.O. Box 33049
Brampton, Ontario
L6S 6A7 Canada

www.wtlipublishing.com

ISBN 978-1-927865-16-3

Printed in Canada and the USA

10 9 8 7 6 5 4 3 2 1

Special Thanks

Thank you, Mom, for caring enough
to give our names such unbelievable strength.
Your love knows no bounds and steadies us all.
You have sacrificed to love at great length.

3

Hi there!!! Don't be shy. Come over and say hello.
You didn't open the cover just to sit back there.
Come closer!

I'm little right now. For sure this is true,
but I have a story to tell.
As you can see, I'm just a baby,
who giggles and smiles really well.

My family's not big. My family's not small.
It's two brothers, my dad and my mom.
Here's all about my brothers and me,
and where our names come from.

I'm Theodore, but don't call me "Teddy."
My mother would make a big fuss.
If she wanted it "Teddy," it would have been,
so go ahead and see if you must.

She isn't being mean. It's a thing with us.
To us, names don't need any masking.
The origins of a name and the meanings behind
get my family excited and asking…

Where is it from? Who gave it to you?
Is it from a king or a queen?
What does it mean? Is it one name or two?
Do you kind of see what I mean?

Here are just a few names we know:
there's Xavier and also Jaiya.
There's Micah, Jauvahn, Loni and Zarah,
Ryan and Angie and Kaya.

Special names and special people,
each beautiful, kind and smart.
Ah, but alas, it's story time,
so let's go ahead and start.

It all began a long time ago.
It was summer of 2003.
My parents were in love—Hey, that's just a fact!
—and they wanted to have a baby.

Yes, a cute baby, a boy or a girl,
so they tried and tried and tried.
But there was no baby for quite some time,
and this came as a surprise.

And then came the news, so hard to hear:
"You can't have a baby at all."
That is what the doctor said,
after they waited for his call.

They wouldn't give up. They never gave in.
In fact, they continued to pray.
They got on their knees and talked to God
and did this every day.

'Dear Father above, if this is your will,
we accept it, no questions asked.
Maybe we won't be a mom and dad.
Perhaps the chance has passed.'

Then that same year brought a surprise,
one that would brighten the day.
A baby was coming, a little boy.
Three cheers! Hip hip hoooooraaay!

Now, remember I told you, names are important.
That's how we started this narration.
So what do you name such a miracle child?
Well, "Matthew-Michael" of course, for appreciation!

Not so easy my friends, it's not just a name.
For that, you can be quite sure.
"Matthew" means "gift from God,"
"Michael" for our daddy,
a name that will endure.

You see what I mean? Names are not just names.
My mommy is onto something wise.
Dad tells a funny story of mom changing the name,
not once, not twice, but ten times.

The power of his name does not stop there.
There's more magic to share here.
Matthew-Michael's middle name comes
from my late Uncle Warren,
a man we all hold dear.

My second other older brother is a wonderful guy,
and, believe me, he has a great heart.
His name is Nathaniel Terrence Afif.
How he got these names is the interesting part.

You will see soon enough there's a common thread
that ties us together real tight.
If you guessed "Nathaniel" means, "gift from God,"
congratulations, my friend. You're right!

But what about Terrence and what about Afif?
Those aren't any regular names.
Well, one was given from our uncle, you see,
the other, from a beautiful game.

Our uncle Victor, a very nice guy,
said Terrence was the name to be given.
But the way he got the other name
will make you wonder how Daddy's still living.

My daddy was at a soccer game
and I don't know how he got this past Mom:
Smarty-pants Daddy spelled FIFA backwards
and I don't know how Mom stayed calm!

So here we are, almost at the end.
I'm not sure about you but it feels strange.
At last, I can tell you about my name
and why my name is my name and
my name CAN'T change!

I was given one truly powerful name:
Theodore Maluke Zayne.
To carry the weight of these powerful names,
we might have to rent a big crane!

I hope you've guessed it and are laughing by now
or when you start to read the next line.
"Theodore," you should have guessed by now,
means "Gift of God" for the third and LAST time!
(That's what Mommy said.)

My other two names have their own story to tell.
With my two brothers and my cousin at hand.
"Maluke" means I'm tender.
"God is gracious" for "Zayne."
Do you see what I mean? Do you understand?

Nathaniel liked Malooka and we liked it too,
but it just wasn't meant to be.
Malooka was the name of a girl we know
and I'm a boy as it's plain to see.

And "Zayne," lovely "Zayne," happens to be
the name Matthew-Michael
and Cousin Angie suggested.
Sad as they were that it's not my first name,
the order they never contested.

So that's the end of my tale and I hope you enjoyed,
and learned a thing or two about names.
Names are powerful things that should be cherished
and their pronunciation, the same.

A name says a lot about who you are,
though the meanings come with different measure.
So take the time to learn and say it right.
That way you won't ruffle any feathers.

Mommy taught and reminds us to be
proud of our full names:
to never settle for anything less.
We three sons say, "We love you,"
and we'll always remember
you and Dad are the best!

www.ingramcontent.com/pod-product-compliance
Lightning Source LLC
Chambersburg PA
CBHW041959100426
42813CB00019B/2930